Who Travels
down this
Narrow Road

Who Travels down this Narrow Road

Henry Pluckrose

Matador
9 Priory Business Park
Wistow Road
Kibworth Beauchamp
Leicester, LE8 0RX
Tel: (+44) 116 279 2299
Email: books@troubador.co.uk
Web: www.troubador.co.uk/matador

ISBN 978 1780880 761

Typeset in 11pt Book Antiqua by Troubador Publishing Ltd, Leicester, UK

Matador is an imprint of Troubador Publishing Ltd

Printed and bound in the UK by TJ International, Padstow, Cornwall

In Memoriam

Henry Pluckrose, much loved teacher and friend

1931 - 2011

ACKNOWLEDGEMENTS

I wish to record my thanks to Henry's sister, Winifred Taylor, for the pen and ink illustrations at the start of each section.

And to Anne Clark, a true friend, who helped Henry greatly during his last weeks, and who worked tirelessly to complete the typing, arrangement and compilation of his selected poems. Her care and attention to detail has been much appreciated in the preparation of this manuscript for publication.

And to the staff of Matador Publishing for the advice and help given through all stages of its production.

Hilary Devonshire

Henry Pluckrose was born on 23 October, 1931. He died on 6 April, 2011. In the months and weeks before he died Henry was in the process of collating his latest book of poetry – this book. "Who Travels down this Narrow Road?", a line taken from the poem 'Harmony', has been produced in his memory.

All his life-time Henry had been attracted to words.

According to legend, as a toddler he wanted to hear a poem before he would eat. As a teenager during the War years his ear for words and music continued to be nourished as a chorister at Southwark Cathedral. Subsequently as a teacher and lecturer, editor, author and raconteur his love of words served him well. He could communicate with three hundred people in a large lecture hall as easily and as personally as to one. An approachable man he liked to be known simply as Henry to his friends, colleagues and children alike.

While working in the field of primary education Henry wrote many books. In some he described his philosophy of open education. In others he sought to help teachers develop their skills, to look outwards, to be creative and imaginative in their work. A large proportion of his publications however were information books written for children but used by adults and children alike. His output was prolific and inspirational and for his work Henry was to become well known at home and overseas.

His favourite hobbies of travel and writing came together in his poetry, 'relaxed verse' he liked to call it. His illness, Parkinson's, diagnosed in 2001, gave him, he said, time to reflect, but his interests, his love of history, his fascination with old buildings, his appreciation of nature and music remained unchanged. Through the creative arts, music and literature he hoped to encourage others, his children, his students, his teachers to share his thirst for knowledge and find enjoyment in the process. He loved visiting art galleries, but he could not paint. "Words are my paintbrush" he said. Putting observations into words was for him a form of play, exploring how words fitted together, enjoying the spoken sounds and cadences.

Learning he felt should be founded on practical experience. Schools should be a base from which the world beyond the gates could be explored. They should be the starting point for discovery, places where, later, the knowledge gained could be researched, developed and recorded creatively through the arts, drama, music and the spoken and written word.

His poetry writing came lately, possibly he thought, due to his medication and this new pastime gave him much pleasure. He was often to be seen with his favourite fountain pen in his ink-stained fingers. He could not be creative on a computer he said, he needed the immediacy of pen on paper.

Some people spoke of Henry as a story-teller and this is true. He loved telling stories, a gift he said, inherited from his father. His poems were to become a poetic diary reflecting the world as he saw it, albeit an increasingly restricted one. Looking, watching, seeing and recording what he saw, was what he did. Writing in situ, 'en plein air' as the artist might say, he highlighted the colours and changes in the world around and tinged his words with his imagination and dreams.

In contrast to the poverty of his early years growing up in Lambeth, he looks back on his 'pleasured childhood' in 'The Return' remembering his choir-boy camping days on Golden Cap, Dorset.

He drew his pictures in words for his readers to experience the scene and share his enthusiasms, hopes, fears, pleasures with him. 'Stop and be refreshed' he says in his poem 'Nature's Ways'.

Many of Henry's poems within this anthology reflect his fascination with existence and passing time. They portray a poignant awareness of his own mortality and a longing for the peace which he now has.

In his last days he spoke of his poem 'Madonna' and said he would like to dedicate it to all his past pupils who wrote to him and remember him.

Henry's exhortation to all not to waste life is hinted at in his poem 'Take Time'. His wish was to motivate even the youngest to use their talents and abilities, to participate to the full.

This his legacy to us.

His last wish was that our memory of him should be 'a celebration of a life lived'. His was indeed a life lived to the full.

Hilary Devonshire, 2011

TIME

Yesterday

I am the sum of all my yesterdays
Each moment of time awake or sleeping
Uniting to add detail, colour, perceptions
To the once embryonic me.

If we are formed by yesterdays, each day is ephemeral,
Its events but shadows
Becoming solid and substantial only when they are past.
And yet I cannot ignore my todays
For each today marks a new moment of the emerging me,
Today's experiences determine the me that is and the me that
is to be.

I am the sum of all my yesterdays
Learning from experience
Taking today into tomorrow
The techniques I need to cope with the vagaries of life.

Words of Time

Now

Now - a fleeting moment, pregnant with possibilities
Now - the start of a dream if
When realised, human life will change forever.
Now - the point at which we accept that years of dedication to a cause
Have failed.
Now - a signpost at the crossroads of life.
Now - a small, mundane, retiring word
When set against its more flamboyant, idiosyncratic colleagues.
Now - divider of what will be and what was.
Now - a word of isolation transforming a word of little weight
Into one of life changing significance.

When

When - rich in time and all its possibilities
When - expresses hope, outpouring of joy
As when a long-time dream is realised.
When - word of closure significant in all its inevitability.

Then

Then - word used to give unity and meaning to fragmented moments
Its unexpectedness often stepping stones from past to present.

Every word is unique
Respect words, be they printed or spoken,
Complex or simple, extravagant or lowly.
The manner in which they are delivered
Speaks of us.

Clock of Life

A solitary bumble bee gathers nectar
From the purple lupin,
Thrusting deep into the flower.
So focussed in his task
That he ignores my falling shadow.
I edge closer and notice the yellow-black coat,
Pollen stained,
Legs misshapen with the detritus of harvesting.

At what hour did this busy creature
Leave the nest?
At what hour return?
A pointless thought.
Only humankind is a slave to minutes, hours, months and years.
Humming, the bee moves unhurried from flower to flower.
The conclusion of his day will be unenforced, natural,
Unbound by ticking clock or confining calendar.

Evermore difficult has it become to live with sensitivity
In this frenetic self indulgent world,
A world where acquisition, pace and speed are accepted
As markers of success.
Stop, stand and stare.
Enjoy the luxury of wonder,
And like the bee be governed
By the natural clock of Life.

Spring 1

In Spring the trees are blossom dressed
Apple competes with pear,
Lilac with cherry
Each demanding our attention,
Urging me to ignore the fading daffodils
The pale narcissus,
Flaming wallflower
Proud tulip tossing its head in the wind.

Sadly the trees soon shed their blossom
Plucked from branch and twig by the freshening wind
They fall, covering with a soft carpet
The grass below.

"It looks as though a wedding's passed this way"
A child remarks (and so it does)
But I more life battered than the child
Reflect that confetti at a wedding
Expresses hope of future happiness.

The message of the trees is more assured.
Today they welcome the warmth of Spring,
Foretell a coming Summer
Fruitful Autumn, rest restoring Winter.
Confetti made by man is tawdry, cheap and paper thin
Too often marks the beginning of the end.
So unlike the trees, whose confetti blossom
Marks the end of the beginning.

Spring II

The apple tree and close-by pear
Are thick with scent and blossom-heavy
Attracting the nectar-seeking bee.
The air is vibrant with the sound of tiny wings.
Pause awhile,
Listen
Wonder
Reflect
Man can build a spaceship,
Construct a bomb.
But cannot make a bee.

July Heatwave

The cloudless skies of yesterday,
The reflective burning sun
Give way to banks of broaching cloud.
Though early, the air is oppressive,
Heavy, humid, draining
Movement has become a tiresome labour.

An unexpected breath of wind.
The bedroom curtains shiver
A single raindrop falls on the concrete patio.
Sucked into its dryness,
The spot expands into a circle
And disappears.

A blue-white flash of blinding intensity
Lights, for a moment, mystical mountains of moving cloud.
A shattering crack, now
The faint rumbles of distant thunder announce
The coming of cooling rain
Which falls in sibilantly whispering sheets.
Pools form on the soil, desert dust dry,
Rivulets pursue each other down patio and path,
Parched flowers wilt, overcome by their watery awakening.

Whipped by sudden wind
The rain falls evermore heavily.
A simultaneous flash and crack
The house shakes as though aware of its vulnerability.
Gusts of wind race across the garden,
The rain now horizontal
Batters trees and bushes.
As suddenly as it had begun, the rain ceases,
The distant thunder lost in the sounds of the town awakening.
The sky lightens
Rolling black clouds give way to fluffy white.

And how shall I remember this July storm?
Not by the thunder, nor by rain,
Rather by the homely scent of dampened grass
The coolness of the air,
The rising sun.
And above all, with thankfulness of sight.

Star-Talk

Near Midnight, Moonless, cloud free.
Wrapped in violet shawl of night
The village, far below, floated,
A pool of orange-white light,
Trembling as if touched with unexpected cold.
Above the arch of Heaven, unifying land and sky,
A blue-black canvas, jewel-touched
Pinpricked with a myriad of stars –
Indeed a Milky Way.
Each star in place and orbit
Ordained when Time began.

The glow of the most distant star
Began its Space Odyssey
Before these Dales were formed
Before amoeba was
Before dinosaurs were
Before humankind could be.
Time, Space, Light, Creation's mystery.
Perhaps that faint dot,
Star-light from distant space,
Began its unending journey across the nothingness of
numberless galaxies
On the very day
When Romulus chose a site, seven-hilled
To build an Eternal City
Or Charlemagne was crowned;
Or when, at Cadiz, Drake, an English privateer,
Burned the Spanish Fleet.

Distant Church clock tells me the hour,
Twelve.
Midnight has come …
                    Midnight has gone
In its brief passage, I have become a
                    Traveller in Time
I had moved
                    but without movement,
The chime took me
From what was Today
Into Tomorrow
And what had been my Today
Became Yesterday.
Life lives in the Time Space of Today
Each life, from birth to death,
A sum of all its Yesterdays.
Tomorrow anticipates
Personal hopes, plans, ambitions.
Measured by star clock's silent chime
These Tomorrows become lost
In the Yesterdays of space.

Near Dawn,
In the East, the Light of Sun,
Tints a cloud free sky.

August Storm

The sky is angry purple-blue.
Heavy darkening clouds dominate the skyline
Seeming to press down on every roof and tree.

A flash. A distant roll of thunder
Encourages Louise, our neighbour's tabby cat,
(The one that owns our garden)
To seek shelter beneath the towering fir.
Determined to keep dry
She speeds to 'her' tree, instinct telling her of coming storm.

Dramatically the light changes,
Dense cloud, now purple- black, tints the flowers.
White alyssum takes a bluer hue,
The trumpets of hollyhock glow, luminously
Even the lawn looks greener in the purple light.

The first hint of rain.
Single droplets, large and pregnant with water,
Each unrelated to its fellow, spatter the concrete path.
The rain quickens, the path disappears
To become a flowing stream.
Louise inches from her tree-cave.
Paws meet water.
Offended at the dampness of her world,
She retreats once more into arboreal darkness.
And waits.

Monsoon-like, rain drums upon my window,
Drops coalesce and race in rivulets down the glass
Anxious to join their fellows on the earth below.

A white flash. A frightening crash.
The storm is overhead.
Louise, provoked by noise beyond her understanding,
Loses all sense of feline dignity
And races, terrified, from sheltering tree
(Clearing with consummate ease
The fence, the thorn-sharp shrubs, the beech hedge beyond)
To her cat flap and safety.

As suddenly as it began, the rain ceases.
The rumbling sky sounds friendly, conversational.
Suddenly white clouds, edged yellow gold,
Promise returning sun.
Leaves, flowers, branches, rain-heavy,
Drip, drip, drip,
Shedding the jewels of water which weigh them down.
Their fall, even and rhythmic,
In nature's final movement in the symphony of storm.
Across a sturdy shrub
A hollyhock lies skewed,
The sole victim of this 'summer weather.'

A ray of sunlight
Louise, dignity restored, strolls down the path,
Ears pricked, tail proudly carried,
She reaches her tree.
Reassured that all is well (and dry!)
She continues her inspection,
The hedge, the greenhouse, the rusting mower
And the gooseberry bed beyond.

A blackbird seeking worms, struts across the lawn,
Head angled,
Summer has returned.

Climate Change?

Sunday morning

Dark mountain-like clouds swirl across the sky.
The weather sullen, threatening, depressing.
Even nature seems ill at ease
Birds, squirrels, foxes (regular visitors)
Have left our garden to find more accommodating homes.
In this half-light, lawn, bush, flower and tree
Have exchanged their shades of green
For funereal purple.

Noon

The atmosphere is one of brooding silence, malign, tense.
Without warning a white flash illuminates my room
An explosive crack shatters the quiet
Then – rain.
Not the soft damp mist beloved of gardeners
But a falling flood, whipped by blustery wind
Into a thick opaque blanket,
Obscuring houses, street, trees, cars ...

Wind and rain, a lowering sky.
It seems as if the clouds are about to envelop all below.
Their malevolence confirmed when rain gives way to hail
Marbles of ice, demanding entry
Throw themselves against roof, window, door.
The lawn so recently a pond
Is transformed into a shimmering mirror.

Twelve fifteen

A sudden stillness
Hail gives way to soft falling rain,
Then to misty dampness
As if the Gods of Wind and Water
Rue their wild excesses.
White cloud replaces black,
Blue sky, white cloud.
A blackbird sits on the fence and sings.
The storm has passed.

Take Time

There's time ahead, I always thought
To take the time I needed
To watch tugs pass along the Thames,
Take train rides unexpected
I stored my time in netting,
As I wasted time with ease
My netting box grew lighter
There's always time
(I always thought)
- But there isn't
-And there wasn't.

PLACES

Below Kilgarren Castle

The River Teifi meanders through the gorge
Its rock face clothed with trees
Which soften and round its sharp contours.
On these sheer cliffs
Ash shares sun and rain with elm,
Sycamore with oak and aspen.
The trees cling to the rocks and to each other
Their exposed roots intertwining like ribbon pattern on Celtic
brooch.
So thick is the vegetation that sunlight fails to penetrate its
depths.
Along the riverbank lie sculptured tree trunks,
Water logged,
Their surface patterned by ever changing light
Reflected.
These crocodile forms cause a momentary shiver to my soul,
A shiver heightened by the grey black bastions of a castle
Brooding on the far cliff face.
These castle stones emphasise earthly power, real and tangible
What peasant owing scutage here would dare ignore his
Lord's command
To lay waste his neighbours' land,
To steal, to kill.

These uninvited thoughts soon fade,
Erased by the beauty of this place,
A place which Turner loved.
And so do I.

Hook

Trimmed, round-topped bank
Encloses resting place of Christian dead
The stones lean forward
Determined, it would seem,
To return to whence they came,
As if remembering their creation
In earthquake, ice and fire
They no longer wish to stand,
As markers of the dead.
Who rests beneath these walking stones
Is hard to tell.
Inscriptions, cracked, moss eaten, crumbling
Confuse fact seeking historian, researcher, descendant.
"These stones have no place here!" (I think)
"They are right to want to go."
Close by tiny chapel, within grassy bank,
Three leafless trees, bent low by prevailing wind
Point the path the stones should follow
The leaning stones, the naked trees
The lowering sky, the thunder clap
So filled my mind, confused my brain
That I would have taken oath
To say
The stones moved ... seawards.

A tap on window of the car, its radio playing softly
And Hilary's voice, so quiet and clear
"Henry, wake up, we're leaving."

Gate

Gate on track through Pembroke hills,
Set in dry stone wall.
Gate, firm shut against intruders.
Gate, five barred, protecting rocky field,
Field where grass competes with sickly gorse
For crevices of soil in which to root.
Against the near horizon, a granite outcrop
Fashioned when the earth was young.

Set high in the Preseli Hills,
This gate a reminder of the New Year yet to come,
A marker on the road of Time.

Ignore the gate,
Continue on your chosen way
Or slip the bolt and seek some other path.

Gate, metaphor of Life.

Twelve Steps in Three Moods

Part 1

Eight steep steps of stone, worn and weathered,
Sit snug inside the churchyard wall.
Here, in this unexpected spot,
Nature displays extravagance uncontrolled
Dressing every tread and riser
In fantasy of dew-dropped gossamer,
Each tiny droplet sparkles, rainbow-rich,
Encouragement to stay awhile
And look.

Eight steep steps of stone, weathered, worn
Touched by soft light of Autumn
Transform into cascading waterfall of blue and white,
The *common* speedwell in full flower
A most *uncommon* sight.

To reach these steps take brambled path.
Four matching moss green steps stand clear,
Climb them.
Across expanse of new-cut grass,
Beneath sweep of woodland oak
A tiny, unexpected church, waits –
For worshippers, a place to hear the voice of God.

Part 2

The builder of this hidden jewel
Lived in a manor house close by.
A man of manners, rich, retiring.
Local squire of good report,
Paid first for clearance of the forest.
Met cost of church and stepped wall,
(Providing way from church to Hall).
Admonished by a sour archdeacon
For ill use of lordly rights,
The Squire replied, with smile endearing,
"Begrudge me not short cut to God!"

Part 3

Stand in mystic quiet of evening
Stand by steep steps, weather worn.
Feel the past surround, enwrap you
Touched by those who went before.
First the monk on route to Baldwas
Did you hear the swallowed swear
As his toe hit the stonework.
See print of foot in dust of tread?
Cry of delight from Lady Jane?
(Her Lord safe back from brutal war.)

Twelve, steep stone steps
From path to churchyard,
Twelve steps weathered, wet and worn,
Steps of speedwell
Steps of gossamer
Steps of present and of past.

Dorset December

Stand high on Kimmeridge Down,
Watch and wonder.
Wild, white topped waves race shorewards
Ordered like Lancers in long forgotten battle
They throw themselves upon the unyielding shore
And like the fallen soldiers, are consumed by Earth.
Across the Bay clouds, purple-black, veil the land,
Dark Nothingness rules all.

Look across the Bay once more
A ray of light from sinking sun illuminates, enlightens,
Questions.
What was unseen is seen,
And that which unknown, known.

Through the centuries, philosophers of all faith and of none
Have woven stories to show the power of light.
"Light", said one, "enables us to see through the darkness of
the Age."
May Christmas be for you a time of light and hope.

Corfe

A fall of wall on man made mound
A slighted keep and ruin.

Stand below this mound, look up
And free your mind with me.
Atop the keep you watch and see
The enemy below.
Voices float through the light of dusk
Laughter, oaths, armours ring,
Unexpected roll of drums.

Lady Bankes betrayed by friend
The castle fell,
King's cause well lost.

The battle returns, crack of musket
Thump of lead and shot
Clash of steel on steel
Screams and curses of the fallen
The smell of death.

The stronghold falls, its treasures sacked
Barbican, keep and curtain walls
Left akimbo on the man made mound
Corfe,
Romantic scene born of the savagery of war.

Madonna on the Lake

Regular visits to Scandinavia between 1970 and 2000 gave me the opportunity to visit hundreds of parish churches – many off the beaten track. My interest in art and architecture was more than satisfied as were the messages they conveyed.

> Here you sit Mary,
> As you have for centuries gone,
> In this little chapel beside the lake.
> Commissioned by some Swedish lord,
> Worked with thoughtful love
> By uncultured peasant hand.
> You lack the sophistication of Nativities
> Fashioned in the Academies of Rome, Venice and Florence
> You are of humble stock
> As is the Christ you offer to us all
> (Bond folk or free)
>
> Here you sit Peasant Madonna,
> Mindful that it was to peasants
> That this birth was first proclaimed.
> The message of the angels
> Still rings loud and clear
> 'Peace on Earth. Goodwill to Men'
> Madonna of the Peasants
> Join us as we say
> 'Amen'

I THINK THEREFORE I AM

Pen is to Paper as Brush is to Canvas

Unthinkingly
My pen skims over paper like a mayfly over water.

Curiously
I ask how it knows how to write.

Deliberately
It avoids the conflicts caused by politics and religion.

Puritanically
It never comments on love or passion.

Consciously
It seems to prefer aspects of tone, texture, colour and form.

Whimsically
Its colours are words which create mind-pictures
For as a brush creates shapes, my pen decorates the mind.

Paradoxically
Its words allow me to be active, independent of my failing
body.

Painlessly
It takes me to where I would go.

Fortunately
My pen still writes legibly.

Irrationally
Commenting on the insubstantial
(Like a mayfly over water)
And reflecting - **me**

Meadowland of Thoughts

Unique,
> The thoughts which germinate and flower
> Within the meadowlands of mind.

At birth
> A meadow unrestricted,
> Extending beyond horizon,
> Lacking ditch, mound, hedge, fence or wall.

Virgin
> Untouched by blade of peasant plough
> Or
> Cut of sharp edge scythe.

Rich Earth
> In which thoughts grow like flowers
> On drained and sunny bank
> Tumbling, cascading in many colours
> Demanding attention, admiration
> Thoughts flower and best seed
> When rooted in the soil of experience
> Moistened by the rain of curiosity.

All too soon
> Each embryo mind, green with seedlings
> Is invaded by the thought-police of convention.
> The unusual, the dissonant are uprooted
> The meadowlands of mind redefined,
> Its borders guarded,
> Lest it be invaded by thoughts of change.

All too often
>Emerging, developing flower thoughts
>Are judged too early
>Thoughts which may reshape
>The world's tomorrows
>Are cut down and burned.

In academic plots
>Divergence is discouraged
>Last season's weakly blooms
>Admired, protected, loved.
>Safe thoughts grow best
>In the soil of complacency
>Fertilised by the ignorance of the stubborn.

Sad am I
>That so many build their hopes for tomorrow's
>children
>On yesterday's yesterday.

Voices

Why do voices invade my thoughts
Emerging from deep recesses of my mind?
Attention seeking, each recalls an element of Time past.

The Sergeant Major's scream at spot on blancoed belt
The trustful 'Daddy' of my daughter's childhood.
The whispered voice of secret love.
The tearful weary voice which said "Diana your sister is dead"

Competing with the personal
I hear voices polite, demanding, indignant
"Spare a coin, Guv"
"Mind the doors"
"You could have told me!"

And on the phone intrusive voices,
Voices I do not recognise.
"I'm ringing to ask …"

How I long for that inner peace,
Born of silence.

The Voice

I walked along the lane today,
The lane we knew when young,
A dappled way of primrose–flower
Of catkins in Spring sun.
Today the lane is lifeless, grey,
All Nature is asleep,
Silence of Eternity it seems,
For the Dead no longer speak.
Then from a swirl of falling leaves
I hear your voice, faint calling,
"Do not weep for me, dear love,
For you I'll wait forever."

I stood alone on packhorse bridge,
The bridge deep in the forest.
The bridge where you first spoke of love
And I was touched with longing.
You took my hand in yours and smiled
We stood – and time – stood still
Perhaps we slept – I do not know –
Spellbound by troll or goblin.
Dark shadows tracked our homeward path,
I feared for our tomorrow.

Today I stand on packhorse bridge
Alone and seared with sorrow,
Above the sky is thunder blue,
Strange darkness clothes the forest.
The tears I shed freeze on my cheek,
Each breath brings pain and aching,
So cold this place that once was warm
I cannot stay here longer.
Then it was your voice I heard
Whispering in my head
"Do not cry for me sweetheart
I'll wait for you forever."

I stood alone where sand meets sea,
By rocks we knew so well.
Here we enjoyed warm summer days
Would that we could still!
A fool I was to take our boat,
Provided for sea sailing.
A keen sharp wind and white tipped waves
We faced with no foreboding.

Across the bay we sailed with ease
The cliffs were our protection
Beyond their arms, the waves grew high
The gale raw, unrelenting.
I saw the terror in your face
I heard your cry for help
You reached for me, I took your hand
Alas you slipped and fell.
I could not reach you where you lay
So lifeless and so still.

I stand beside your resting place
In churchyard high on cliff
I hate myself for what I've done
Where could I find forgiveness?
Before I leave this lonely spot
I take the ring, a silver band
The ring you bought from gypsy.
A token of your love for me,
A love to last forever.

I dug a hole in soft grave mound
Your ring I hid within it.
A token of the love I've lost,
I've placed beside you darling.
And then the whisper came again
Your voice both faint and clear.
"Do not mourn for me, dear love
I'll wait for you forever."

Orison for the Newly Born

Recently come into the world
Where people are measured by their wealth and possessions
New born child, what would I wish you?

Not material success for the cost is too high
The fight for status, recognition, popularity
Warps the personality, making enemies of erstwhile friends.
Some may wish you academic achievement
Where self indulgence grows with research completed
Bringing with it an intellectual arrogance that is spiritually
undermining.
Is there value in knowing the minutiae of a subject
That you can only explore it
By yourself?
Take, but not to excess.

My first hope is that you are blessed
With sound mind and body.
On this your life depends.
Good health will enable you to prosper in these sad and angry
times.
Remember that time is life.
Wasted hours, days, weeks, months, years
Can never be regained.

Do not be too solemn,
But bring a sense of humour to all that you do.
Seeing the ridiculous in most things human almost guarantees
survival!

I would have you compassionate
A rare quality, often despised.
Our aggressive and competitive age
Holds that turning the other cheek
Or walking the second mile
A sign of weakness.
This is not so.
To disassociate yourself from the easy option requires courage
And points to one who does not tolerate blind shallow
conformity.

Like every child you have unique gifts.
May your individuality flower.
Offer to those around you a vision of the possible,
A possible beyond the everyday and commonplace,
A vision which rejects the corruption of self interest.

Finally I would wish you to appreciate
That nothing is gained by conflict –
Between neighbours,
Between nations,
Within families.
And that it is easier to make war
Than to make peace.

May you be blessed with a loving personality.
For love of our fellow human beings
And love of the environment we all share
Is central to a life of contentment.
Amen.

Loves

I love to hear
Sounds which seduce the ear
Blackbird telling me of his delight at rise of sun.
Mozart cadenza from passing car,
The even throb, throb, throb, of heavy rain,
Sighs of waves retreating,
Key in lock which tells of safe return
Silent snow,
Tick of clock in empty room.

I love to smell
The scent of dew on fresh cut grass,
Lavender blossom
The 'tasted' smell of new baked bread,
The green freshness of the countryside.
Aromatic fragrance.
The lingering dustiness of old books.

I love to touch
Dry garden soil, as it crumbles between the fingers
The tickle of sand beneath toes
The rough wool of a well-worn sweater,
The wondrous fingers of a new born baby,
Hot water foamed with perfumed oils.
Clean, glistening hair.

I love to taste
The sharpness of lemon,
Hot chocolate when the night is cold.
Peppermint toothpaste
Roasted chestnuts, fire flavoured.
The warm comfort of cold milk,
The salt of relieving tears.

I love to see
A welcoming smile,
To marvel at purple storm clouds over lake and estuary,
Ice fronds on bare branches,
Trees, silhouetted against the sky, their very nakedness a thing
of beauty.
Stars, patterning the heavens,
Order in haphazardness.

Advancing years may cause these loves to fade or vanish
Replaced by others more appropriate to my years.
Who knows, my love might be
A plate of kippers, a glass of ginger ale or a smile at me.

The Bridge

A lifeless giant lies across the narrow valley
Natural bridge over fast flowing brook.
Stripped bare by wind and sun
Its branches spring skywards, space leaping from its solid trunk
Strands, once roots, cobweb dressed, hang low
Seeking security of Mother Earth.
Weather scoured this whitened skeleton still proclaims life.

Look close at each weathered root and branch, a paradox.
A paradox, for in its barrenness life flourishes.
Insects burrow through its bark, voles make their nests
Birds perch high above the path, singing of love and challenge.

A living giant lies across the narrow valley
Showing that in death there is life,
My companion stirs, anxious to go
But I am loath to leave …

ETERNITY

The Oaks

On distant ridge six stout oaks stand
Sharp silhouettes on mottled sky.
Saplings they were, planted with care, by Squire John
Whose family held these lands
When Edward (Peacemaker) was King.

Six English oaks with space to grow,
Majestic their response,
Season upon season they transformed
The bleak starkness of the ridge
Encouraging the eye to see beauty in bleakness,
Lacelike traceries of winter branches
Touched by green to welcome Spring.
Full foliage of Summer followed.
These seasons precede the climax of
Autumn's dress of orange, red.

Dawn,
Mid-winter sun illuminates the ridge.
Imperceptibly night retreats
The oaks,
Clear against last evening's blood red sky
Are lost in all concealing mist.
Slowly mist gives way to sun,
Though narrow twists remain.
Like bridal veils they dress the oaks
Sun sparkling canopies confirm the slow turning of the year.

Silhouettes on distant ridge
Six oaks stand
Uniting earth and sky.

The Fool

Yesterday we dressed the tree
As we have done for many a Christmas past.
Memories from childhood filled my thoughts ...

Trafalgar Square and wood rich smell of Oslo's tree,
The wreaths of yew and pine on friendly Devon doors
Sparkling in response to light from exploding bomb and shell.
And I recall my days in Southwark choir
When, hair neat-combed and cassock dressed,
We processed to greet Sir Thomas Guy,
Carolling, his blessing gained
We took angelic music toward
Waiting room, reception space and lift.

Today the lights on our tree tremble, glow
Shedding new colour on bell and bauble,
Golden train and silver trumpet,
Wooden doll, sleigh, soldier.
Carols play on tape and disc
In keeping with tradition
Alas, my days of treble are no more
My poor hum a toneless thing
To greet this child, our new born King.

Until Epiphany our tree will stand,
Recording Christmas and the fading year.
How nostalgic, sentimental this must seem
To stockbrokers who live in Frinton Green!
"Only a fool," I hear them say,
"Would elevate the humble pine
Above possessions, 'wealth sublime'."

And yet I do
For such a fool am I.

Simply Poppies

July 1917 London

A remembrance, the poppy, for those who die in war,
The petals bright red, like blood fresh shed,
The stamen mourning black,
The flower, high on whiskered stalk
Gently bows her head
As if in unexpected prayer
Perhaps the whispered words of wind
Spoke of new dead on Somme or Marne
Of life-taking mud in Flanders

While poppy drinks the light of sun
The leaves from which it grows
Tighten, form a cushion,
A wreath to mark a death.

The poppy flowers but briefly
Only two weeks have passed
Since London's streets, parks, squares, gardens
Shone, danced in glorious red.
Where flowers flamed, fat seed pods form
Their shape like kettle drum.

These, the drums on shire horse flanks
Beat the call to battle.
The soldiers followed, trance-like their step,
Its rhythm told them not to fear,
Advance to certain victory, untouched, unscarred.

High Summer 1917 Flanders

Wild, the rain drenched poppies grow
In the cold fields of Flanders.
A graveyard this, of hopes and dreams
Shortened lives and grieving,
Dreamers from many lands died here
All fought, they thought, to save
A way of life, their Nation's rights.

King, Czar, Kaiser, those who ruled,
Explained at length why young men must die
To satisfy a war machine,
Their bodies a token, left to rot
Their shrouds rich Flanders clay.

Robe-rich priests prayed with them
Before they went to fight.
Blessed them, shrived them, comforted,
And told them (should they fall)
Of Eternal Life for all.

Only the poppies listened,
And, red as Advent's cope,
They flower in June in 'no man's land'
Proclaiming life remembered,
Reflecting on life lost.

In dank, bleak, dark November
When poppies rest in earth,
We pin an emblem on our coat
And share a common thought
That poppy, war weary flower of blood,
Becomes a flower of hope.

Light of Faith

The Abbey of Thornton, East Anglia
In the Year of Our Lord 1303

Testing days of Lent now over
And Good Friday rituals done
Saturday spent in quiet meditation
Death defeating, Mary's son.

Monks who give their lives to Thornton
Create traditions of their own,
Each Lent, things of beauty hidden.
At saints' shrines no candles glow.

Novice monks are now exhausted
In the light of moon prepare
Abbey Church for celebration
Solemn High Mass, joyful prayer.

Preceptor stands at door of cloister
Easter 'Hodie' to sing
A thank you to their God in Heaven
For the victory of their King.

Bell struck loud to wake the sleepers,
Drowsy monks their eyes tight closed
Stumble round the cot they sleep in
Looking in the dark for clothes.

In bleak gloom of dim lit cloister
They stood waiting, did not see
Brother Peter – swamped by cassock,
Brother John's just reached his knee.

Now they moved in slow procession
Down steep steps into the church
Chanting in a modern setting
Gregory's Litany, verse by verse.

In the gloom they passed the Chancel
Shadowy was the altar cross
With relief reached stalls in Quire,
'Neath the vaulted roof embossed.

Now came the moment of great drama
Abbot dressed in vestments gold
Called each novice, taper glowing
"Roll back dark sin, Christ's light behold."

Becoming and Unbecoming

Time became
Our universe emerges from primeval matter
A concept far beyond my understanding
Planets and stars spin in the expanse of space
Bound by gravity unseen
And follow their prescribed orbits round the sun.

And Earth became
Its birth pangs, retrospective
Continue across eons of incomprehensible time
Turbulence from within, monstrous labour pains
Fashion valley and mountain
Plain, plateau and gorge
Continent, lake, sea, ocean.

Then Life became
Grasses and frond forests emerged
Amoeba, ammonite, worm, gnat,
Great flying birds, dinosaurs
Each a marvel of evolution.

And unbecame
Not every form survived,
Natural forces from within earth's core,
Heat from an oppressive sun,
Century upon century of ice and frost,
Caused their extinction
But some remain with us still
The crocodile, the coelacanth, the tortoise.

And Man became

Homo Sapiens came and sought to rule the earth
Ordering Nature and her ways
Forgetful of the unbecomings of time past.
Will man remain
Or through stupidity and stubbornness of will
Leave Earth
To crocodile and tortoise?

Passing Light

Stand high on this naked cliff.
Across the Bay and glass-topped sea
Dark silhouettes of mist-frocked hills
Float in dying light.

Like silent thieves, both sea and sky
Steal colour from the setting sun
To leave a fine wrought line of gold
Along horizon's length.

No fear we show at loss of sun
Certain of its return.
A sign of an Eternal Pulse
And the insignificance of Man.

NATURE'S TOUCH

The Ash

High against the sky line,
Its lower branches reaching down to hill-side track,
A solitary ash.
A playful wind snipes at its few remaining leaves,
They fall, transforming the narrow stream into a moving
carpet,
Yellow, red and golden brown.

Autumn, early evening,
Fading light, beneath a cloud free sky,
Gives purple tint to broad sweep of Preseli Hills,
A year has turned since last I came this way.
Again the Ash will face the storms of Winter
And as in times past
Respond to Nature's pattern,
If Autumn's passed then Spring's not far away.

Weeds Revealed

Blue sky replacing rain clouds,
I decided to garden.
Choosing the bed
I noticed they looked up at me
And seemed to smile,
Those weeds.

I ignore their greetings
Ruthlessly I clear the ground for flowers,
Rooting up the intrusive weeds.

Some minutes later
I return with busy-lizzie and marigold
And notice all the weeds I've missed.
I put down my plants new purchased
To examine with greater care and fresh eyes
The weeds which still clung to the soil.
I see for the first time
The beauty of their tiny flowers,
The exquisite filigree of their leaves,
All reminders of the mystery of creation.

I look again
On one minute flower
A butterfly languishes,
Close by, a honey bee seeks nectar.
Respected by Nature, those weeds,
Even by the snails (who much prefer my primula).

My thoughts race on.
Those weeds I have so long despised
Cost no money,
Need no human hand to plant or tend
Resist rain, snow, ice and sun.

Now I understand
Why weeds smile!

The Magic Road

Beech trees grace this road
Making it a witness to an age long gone
When gardens and parklands were created
For posterity, (not instant satisfaction).

Look down from Bradbury Rings,
A Celtic fort.
Two lines of tall beech trees
Unite horizon with horizon
Their closely interwoven branches form a tunnel
Concealing the busy road which runs beneath.

The branches high above resemble towering vault of medieval
church,
No plainsong echoes through this aisle
Only the raucous cry of wheeling evening rooks
Tell Vespers.
Below, around the twisting roots,
A carpet of flowers, anemone and dandelion.

The trees which form the pillars of this natural aisle
Are lichen mottled, silvery grey,
A light green tint of bursting buds
Hints at Summer yet to come.
Sufficient leaves there are to cause the road to shimmer,
Turning coarse asphalt into glistening fairy waterway.

Sadly the trees have not escaped man's tender care.
Each is seared and scarred where trunk gives way to branch.
The woodman's stumps remain,
Sculptured by nature into gruesome figures
Troll, Hobgoblin, malevolent Dwarf,
Pixie and Puck are here,
Their bodies twisted and deformed.

Silently through the dark hours,
They patrol road and fort,
As they did when Celtic poets in Bradbury Ring
Wove stories of the night
And told of the cleansing light of day.

Visit this road at dusk
Feel darkness come, watch the shapes emerge
Then hurry homewards
And leave this magic place
A place which Nature's Spirits have made their own.

Moving Earth

Moonlight, pale, watery,
Filtered by banks of drifting cloud
Momentarily lights the ground around an evergreen.
From its bole, squat, smooth barked, twigless
Grow six branches,
Thicker by far than those of most town trees.
High above, each branch bears an island
A canopy against a sea-sky of blue night,
A canopy denying light to everything below.

In light-less moonshine, eyes deceive
And mind, imagination freed, responds.
An instant ... and eyes see what there is not,
To give shape, form, colour
To things blind mind has seen.

A glimpse of moon,
Around the bole, firm earth heaves,
Slips, slides upon itself, falls back,
The movement of tumultuous waves upon unfriendly ocean.

A second glance and all is clear
There is a battle ground
Where serpents from worlds long past,
Writhe and wrestle grip and thrust
The coils which bind snake to snake
Are thick as wrestlers' thighs,
Their grey-green scales slashed, scarred.
A mortal witness, here I stood and watched the Titans' battle!

My mind tells me this cannot be,
No Gorgon head whose every hair is stinging snake
Sleeps here on village green in Dorset.

Suddenly the moon, cloud clear,
Lightens writhing earth.
My eyes no longer do deceive
My snakes?
Tree roots in earth!

Gentle Confrontation

A colourful jay,
Pink breast blending into red-brown back,
Wings touched with white and blue
Explores the frozen grass for worm and grub,
Unsuccessfully.
Now he stands with angled head
Bright eyed, clean beaked
Puzzled at winter's unwelcome coming.

From ivy-covered fence
A magpie watches,
Cautiously,
His green blue coat, white shirted,
Shines in the early evening sun.

Each bird ignores the other,
Though both unsettled by rival presence.
A moment of indecision,
And Magpie joins Jay.
One step towards Jay and the Magpie freezes
Then, like partners in a barn dance
The Magpie, with unexpected thrust of wings,
Rises to the Jay's light hop
Before falling back to earth.

The spontaneous dance
Looks practised
Step, leap, wings aflutter

These courtesies come to sudden end
Without a bow or curtsey.
A harsh cry from now angry jay
Calls down his mate.
Then follows confrontation, second magpie landing next to
first.
Eyes fixed in threatening stare
Each bird assesses rival.
Why should a quarrel follow
Their formal pas de deux?
Then surprised by sudden blast of bitter wind,
Both pairs retreat to branch of leafless oak
And perch close, side by side, in harmony.

The drama over,
The lawn returns to its unmoving winter whiteness.

Christopher

I look at all the cats I meet
And wonder how they pass their days
Do felines have a life like ours
And toil to earn their daily pay?

I think they do, so there must be
Cats who type, compute, police
Sweep streets, teach, give therapies
Provide those things which cats need.

You know because I've told you
(It's never in the Press)
That hidden deep in Whitehall
Is the 'Cat and Paw Commission'
An arm of the Government.

The team of cats who work here
Are of the Upper Crust
Cats with links to noble names
(I'll name them if I must)
These are those who wield the power
Whose meow is one of trust.

Among these cats of influence
Is HE who lives next door
A cat with roots in stately home
And links to Bush and Blair.
You know that Chris is special
By studying his gait

On padded paws, head proudly held
Tail high, back straight,
He takes himself to business impeccably dressed
His shirt front white as falling snow,
His waistcoat neatly pressed.
He works for around an hour each day
A job of some importance
He sells cat bonds and stocks and shares
(On line) and life assurance.
I am so proud to know, first hand
This cat with manners gracious
He even smiles if I approach
(Providing he needs feeding!)

To Jane who cares for Christopher
I have a simple warning
Take care lest he decide
To take your household over.
Should this ever come to pass
No front door will you use
The cat flap will be widened
Your meals will come from frozen tins
(Fish, chicken chunks and biscuit).
A bed with mattress will be replaced
With blanket on the table
And when HE goes on holidays
You'll be left to thoughtful neighbours.

So take advice
Respect Chris-cat
A puss of much potential
I hear from friends
His next big job
Is reorganising the Prudential.

The Survivors

Mid day chill of early winter
Grey, bare twigs point upwards
Through the debris
Of summer border.
Frost stiff, they stand like lancers in military square.
Birds seek food
A blackbird busies himself
Turning over the decaying wood chips,
Hopeful of finding snail or worm.

A sparrow, noisier and less industrious
Perches high on cherry tree.
With head to one side,
He studies a fat-ball
Hanging on a branch below.
Then with expertise learned in warm summer days,
(Days spent in company of agile tit,)
The sparrow swoops
And lands, claws outstretched, secure.

He begins to eat, scraps fall below
Where a grey blue pigeon
Gratefully clears seeds and fat which fall around him.
The birds are hungry.
The garden, Nature's food store, is bare
The clowns and the songsters of summer
Have become rude scavengers
Spring seems so far away.

Nature's Ways

Here, where surrounding hills fall gently, smoothed curved,
Here, where sheep-grazed downland, gives way to tended
field
And to marshy scrub,
Here, where springs of water, crystal-clear
United form a stream,
Here, you will find paths and tracks from near and far
Meet, touch, intermingle, linger ...
Reflect, like old friends new met and loathe to say goodbye.
Here you will see
Solitary hiker, lovers, children, parents,
As they pause, feel Nature's calming touch,
And contemplate which path to follow.
Man, town-tied, town-worn, deafened, blinded
Will find relief and healing along every country track.

Choose your path –

> Cross yellow-brackened moor,
> through green-grey dappled woodland,
> by edge of sea at turn of tide,
> or lonely tarn on rock strewn hill

Follow it and be refreshed.

Harmony

Who travels down this narrow road?
No one has passed while I have rested here
Beside this wall.
The wall is old, fashioned in grey blue stone, moss covered,
Its broad flat top pricked with undernourished grass.

With my eyes,
I follow the wall into the distance as it swings right
To become the balustrade of ancient three arched bridge,
This seamless transformation is a tribute to the mason's art
Giving sympathetic symmetry to wall, road and bridge,
Three in one!
Beneath the bridge a restless river
Chatters over its stone gravel bed
Protesting in watery whispers at the cutwaters which break its
flow.

On the far bank, beech, oak and elm compete for space
Leaning low, rejoicing Narcissus-like at their reflections.
Impervious to such vanity
The river steals the colour to itself
Mixing green with blue of sky and mottled pink with drifting
cloud
Perhaps on Autumn days the river runs deep red
Or Winter white when hoar frost paints the trees.
Here is a place of beauty
Where Man's intrusion upon Nature has led
Not to conflict but to pleasing harmony.

MEMORIES

Second Sight

Alone I stood on high cliff path,
A spot I know so well.
Here many hours of boyhood spent
Learned much of Nature's lore.
The deadly swoop of kite on prey,
Streamlined gannet's plunge
Drift of gull in thermal stream,
The rising song of lark.

I looked down on the wave-washed rocks
And then across the Bay,
Familiar was this all to me –
And yet there was a change.
I felt as though I was new born
My eyes began to see –
Beauty in the common place
In sky, on land, at sea.

Now with more enquiring eyes
I watched night's slow advance
Draining colours, greying gorse,
Unseeing turned to seeing.

Beyond the Bay, a range of hills
Defied the spread of night
Wrapped in mist, their sun topped peaks
Float in deepening sky.
I found my path and made for home
Aware of all I'd missed –
Those wondrous things at which I'd **looked**
And oh, so rarely, **seen**.

The Return

This my journey down the years
To days of pleasured boyhood.
But how could this field, rough and brown
Carry me into dreamland?
The field has been so long neglected
Passing time left it untouched
Tall banks of nettle mark it clearly
Their white flowers, made invisible
By butterflies' peacock coloured wings.

Along one side a ditch rock hard,
Dry in summer
Where I watched fox cubs play
The field, pock marked with the hillocks of moles
Was hunting ground for smooth snake, newt and toad.
Tall grasses whispered in the wind
Their thick, coarse stems alight with jewelled flowers.
Shimmering leaves of five tall aspen sheltered the burrow of
sleeping Celt.
Legend said in misty nights he will appear
To bring misfortune to all he meets.

My mind confused. This place I know but how can then be
now?
In the centre of the field I saw our camp, its tents and gear
I saw myself and all my friends,
They seemed to grow from burning fire
Whose flames licked skyward, red ember rich,
Smoke bitter to my taste,
Blue-grey wisps drifted, thinned then vanished.
A parable of living.

The wisps were like those human friends, once vibrant, gently
moving
They dimmed and like the smoke, were lost to me forever.
Spellbound I stood, music filled my ears,
Songs of yesterday awakening the past
Shaping soul and being.

This my journey down the years
Return to pleasured boyhood.

Final Rest

Blood red the Sun
Blood red the windless sea,
Blood red the empty drifting hulk,
Once man o' war was she.

No life on board, no man, no beast
No shanty man to sing
No cries or shouts, from boys aloft
No blessing from a priest.

The horizon's flickering line of fire
Enfolds the hulk with flame
While mermaids from the far Azores
Prepare her watery grave.

Beneath full moon of azure blue
The hulk moves as if directed
To disappear beneath the waves
To Neptune's watery kingdom.

Six months ago I trod this path
When all was red and fiery
Tonight the world is bitter cold
No place for creatures living.

Blue-white the dunes of golden sand
White-blue the grass once green
Blue-white the feathery falling snow
On spume of racing wavelets.

Cold white the light of cloud tossed moon,
Ghost like, insubstantial
Crewed by sailors long since dead.
All seeking rest eternal.

Distant thunder murmurs long
Like guns in antique battle
Beneath the sea it's quiet at last
Peace is their memorial.

Murmurs from the Past

Around the small village green.
Before the church,
In the shadow of the Baptist Chapel,
Along Mill Lane,
Here you can feel the spirits of Llangwm long gone.

One cannot see them
For they are not of this world
The space they once possessed is now enjoyed by the living.
These spirits – from the babe to the aged,
Travel from the vibrant land of the quick
Into the shadow lands of memory.

What can these shadows hope for?
To be recalled in later years through family legends,
Or discovered as a name in national archive.
Captured prosaically on yellowing photograph
In Edwardian newspaper cutting,
Or in handwriting on postcard, note or letter.
We found Martha John, a powerful shadow, this,
In picture, story, photograph and legend.
Even in a notice, framed, in Parish Church.

Half remembered, half forgotten
These shadows of our family past
Touch us, their living descendents,
Silently warning, encouraging, cajoling.
Showing us through their lived lives
The price of success or failure.
For as it is with Nations
So it is with families.
Inner strength comes from drawing upon the past.
Not in using it to create a myth
To justify our present.

Strange Encounter or Seeing is Believing

It was in Salisbury City
A day in mid-July,
I chanced upon a coffee shop
My thirst to satisfy.

The coffee shop was crowded,
With few seats for the taking,
We found a table by the door
Next to two ladies, talking.

I could not but overhear
Conversation most unusual.
A bus at twelve o'clock they'd catch
Then explore a village, rural.

Spellbound, I memorised their plans
To spend time in fields and ditches,
Places rich in snail and slug ...
These two were active witches!

Both looked furtively around
To me gave glance of warning,
With lowered voices they spoke on,
Told of things strange and haunting.

One said "I think that May is best,
Spring weather suits the spirits.
Last night's coven raised but one –
A sea captain called Fillip."

The second witch (if witch she be),
Gave credence to the story,
"He spoke Old Norse and made remarks
Some wise, some crude, some sporty."

"I hope he will some day return
With smell of rum and ocean.
His coat dripped sand where'ere he trod
Room swayed with wave-like motion."

The conversation then returned
To thoughts of the agenda
"I think we'll choose the 13th day,
It's so easy to remember."

Hilary returned at last,
Refreshments filled the tray
I told her of the witches there
She observed I must be fey.

I knew my story she'd reject,
She thought my words semantic.
She paused and failed to hear
A decision most romantic.

"Old Sarum is the place to meet
Hecate will come from Blackpool
Across the horned moon she'll fly
To drum beat, long and soulful."

By now I'd gathered both their names
Esmerelda and Lurchember
I listened on, now all agog,
I'd so much to remember.

"Last night failed." 'Lurchy' observed,
"Because we're less than seven.
Our group's too small, we must enrol
New blood, at least eleven."

"We meet next year in Mildred's barn,
Each fourth Friday at six.
Her husband Reggie may 'appear',
She says he's crossed the Styx."

"Agatha has gone abroad,
Hermione shows no promise.
Stephanie is always late
Though we can rely on Vomit."

"I've spoken to a Don at Kings,
A worthy witch, but male.
His seminars are always full …
And therein lies a tale!"

We ate and drank before we left
The witches were still talking.
Before them, showing month of May
The Diary, me supporting.

We crossed the square and reached the car,
And here you'll think I'm dreaming,
On wing mirrors (both left and right)
Sat cats black, loudly purring.

These cats confirm my words – agree?
Witches they were most surely
I looked again, the cats were gone …
I felt bereft and poorly.

Hilary silently drove me home
To Dulwich via Merton
Tomorrow doctors I will see,
To test my ears, I'm certain.

Encounter

*Clapham, once a prosperous village on the outskirts of
London, was the home of Henry Thornton (1760 to 1815).
Thornton was a leading campaigner against the slave trade,
which was abolished in the British Empire in 1833.*

Early evening, late November in the year just passed,
Beyond the Common
The Parish Church sits framed by oak and elm.
Close by, 'The Triangle' three terraced rows of Georgian
houses
Swamped by the accretions of more recent days.

This evening, church, triangle and trees
Are wrapped in yellow swirls of all concealing fog.
Commuters and school children hurry home
Blurred shadow shapes in mysterious light.

A figure, antique clothed, emerges from the church
And would speak with me.
I see him still top hatted, wearing morning coat,
                                cravat at throat,
"You live here freely now? No longer one enslaved?
Tell me of success."

Some hidden force compels an answer.
I speak of overcrowded housing, unemployment,
                          discrimination, in-born hate
And add, "But I am free."

He smiles and presses a card into my hand
I glance up and see him gone
A shadowy shade in thickening fog
Who wanted words with me.

His card I held in my hand still
I read then read again
The name on the card
"Henry Thornton, Banker"
I knew at once I'd somehow met
A ghost of Clapham past ...
A fervent anti-slaver.
The fog within my mind then cleared.
He'd asked me questions – cos I'm black.

The Living Thames

Thames, haunt of my childhood.
Along your Embankments I ran and galloped,
Racing coal coaster, barge and pleasure craft
En route for Tower Bridge and the Sea.

Seventy years have passed.
Now with more discerning eyes
I watch you ebb and flow,
Follow wavelets in wash of busy tug,
See them glisten in sunlight,
Hear them sigh as they break
Against your confining walls.

A length of wood bobs by,
My mind floats free.
I stand, bewitched as ghosts of London past appear
Shimmering on your surface.

A proud Centurion, newly come from Gaul
Tosses a dinarius into Horseferry Marsh
Praying that Neptune calm his fretting horse.

The image fades.
Now comes royal barge with clockwork rhythmed oars.
Its cargo royal, a disgraced Queen,
Destined for prison cell and execution block
In Henry's Bloody Tower.

A ripple and a cloud across the sun,
Revealing ancient knight and youthful page
In boat bedecked in blue and gold
Their destination Richmond.

Close by, at St. Peter's Watergate, stands a Georgian Dandy
Bewigged, powdered, snuff on thumb,
Neat calf, richly suited.
His quest? A waterman to ferry him to Vauxhall,
Where he can while away the night
In sensuous wickedness.

A darker shadow, that of bomber plane,
Its silhouette black upon your water.
I see my family hurrying to shelter,
Hear guns, relive my fears.

Big Ben strikes the hour,
My years return.
But you flow on,
Carrying the past into the present
To some unimaginable future.

Thames, river of my childhood
And my grandchildren's tomorrow.

Index of Titles